salmonpoetry

Diverse Voices from Ireland and the World

the arts council
an chomhairle
ealaíon

funding
literature

Beautiful Lofty Things
Cahal Dallat

Published in 2022 by
Salmon Poetry
Cliffs of Moher, County Clare, Ireland
Website: www.salmonpoetry.com
Email: info@salmonpoetry.com

ISBN 978-1-915022-07-3

Cover and interior photographs: author's own
Cover Design & Typesetting: *Siobhán Hutson*

Printed in Ireland by Sprint Print

Salmon Poetry gratefully acknowledges the support of
The Arts Council / An Chomhairle Ealaíon

For Anne-Marie, Matthew, Ruth, Simon, Sonya,
Elliot, Sophia, Phoebe and Luca

Contents

Foreword

No ideas but in things
WILLIAM CARLOS WILLIAMS

Not that I spend all my time *thinking of things*, lofty or otherwise. Haven't, officially, been a collector of *things* since the break-up of my childhood museum, comprising one mediaeval-looking pair of handcuffs, amethyst from Achill Island, sea-urchin fossils, a stopped fob watch, granite from Dublin's exploded Nelson's Column, tephrite Vesuvius rock, a USSR cuckoo clock, and hair from Arkle's tail (the last, I now acknowledge, probably the whim of a droll uncle). Though I still slept with a genuine 1798-uprising cutlass under my bed for years, even after I brought my wife and children back on visits to the parental home years later. The sword hangs, now, in the Town Museum.

Possessions dwindled as I left home with a kitbag of dreams: inevitably, perhaps, given an Irish linguistic inheritance that omits the verb *to have*, that doesn't recognise possession *of* things, though possession *by* talismanic objects remains a real possibility still.

I live uncluttered now, apart from books and, all over the house, musical instruments. But I've gradually come to see how many poems spring from, or touch on, sundry objects, whether in loft and cellar, on shelves, in a desk drawer (gallery cards, tickets, photos), even favourite paperbacks stacked sideways on an otherwise orderly bookshelf. And have slowly come to recognise the joy of stuff as well as *lacrimae rerum*, to realise how many people, how many aspects of existence, near or chronologicaly/geographically distant, connect through the tangible artefacts around me.

A little short of a history of the world in 100 objects: a short object-inspired personal history, perhaps.

CD

MYCRO

Hard to grasp now how impressed
we were once by this miniscule gem:
a mail-order-shipped spy micro-camera
from South Dakota – why would a mag
as banal as my father's monthly *Practical
Householder* with *hints for picket-fencing*
and bearded plywood-Santa templates
even advertise such KGB-ish gizmos?

How'd they commodity-code it
on the USPS customs form? Maybe
espionage was a regular check-box,
legitimate Cold-War hobby?

Lumbered every outing with Leica,
flashgun, canisters, cloud-filter, fisheye,
sundry wide-angles and *Leningrada* light meter,
the intricacy of this palm-size space-age
miracle'd dazzled him.
                              But with
folded Cyrillic instructions still crisp
inside the tan leather case, seems
he never did get to snap those
blueprints, conning towers,
the unorthodox beards and gumboots
in an October quayside bar.

YOU MUST REMEMBER THIS

The fundamental things apply
HERMAN HUPFIELD, *As Time Goes By*

Zero memorable in that tourist-town
chaos afternoon: this jar,
some tiles, no *emigré* gin-joint
to walk into, to chant *Allons, enfants!*
over *über alles*, no, just the predictable *souk*,
haggle, persistence and push,
a pestilence of flies.

         And the taxi-driver,
our son's folded puschair
unlashed on his luggage rack,
chugging the three of us in a raddled
Simca 1000 a mere five-hundred
metres give-or-take from the port
to rip us off in *dirhams*: predictably,
as we must have looked all
of our twenty-two years.

         But
you will remember this – and it's
somewhere in attic albums too: you,
short-haired for once, in pale-blue
shirt-sleeves, long ruched
red skirt, Morocco-leather
flipflops, lost
        in thought
at a ship's white-glossed rail
as we sail out of the blue into sere stark heat
and light
      oceans
          continents
             a world ahead of us.

SHAKIN' ALL OVER

Not only did I get all the Pirates'
autographs, the summer Screaming Lord Sutch
hit the Baptist's August dance-tent,
but I got to riff on the backing band's
baritone sax — inches taller than I was —
to sit at Frank Farley's drums (Cattini
had joined the Tornadoes by then,
Mick Green the Dakotas) and got to
restring John Weider's guitar
(before he, too, left for the Animals)

but I woke that next bright morning
to find Kidd and the gang funambulating
on our front railings like the Beatles in *Help!*
(the Monkees wouldn't do their *Hey, Hey!*
until after Christmas) insisting my father phone
the 'vicar' — Father O'Brien — and organise
taxis to take them to the Civil Airport, not that
my father was the dance-hall promoter (despite
his *Blue Serenaders* career), but the local
teacher's ever the go-to guy in small towns.

By September I'd polished Mick Green's
E-minor riff from *Shakin'*: Jim Reeves,
Englebert, and the The Four Tops were
all riding high in the charts. *Can't*
                              remember
if I cried/when I read about the Road
Traffic Incident on Bury New Road
but I switched to alto sax and traded
Johnny's scribbled flourish for three thousand
Confederate dollars with signatures
a hundred years worthless by then.

MY WAY

Wind it this way —
from Aunt Ena's jewellery case you'd get
Brahms' plinking *Lullaby* or Rosas's
Over the Waves — this one has Frank's
braggadocio, his *n'grette-rien*,
the *did what I had to do* that
emboldened Thatcher's children.

And I'm suddenly in summer
third-floor offices, late,
shaking to the open-mic vocalist
and booming bass from a Hoxton bar
below, doomed to segué, at every
evening's end, into a lachrymose
Don't Cry for me Argentina.
                              Winding it
anti-clockwise *Paternoster*-like might yet
undo those hideous backward decades:

but try this. Do it my way.
Fast-forward and it's the Gypsy Kings'
A mi manera and we're into
crevettes *al fresco* with Monica
at Mezza Luna, Juan les Pins.
                              It's Easter
with Ruth in her new Naf-Naf shirt,
and Monsignor Quixote's still next door
at Baie des Anges.
                    Clear in this light
to whom tomorrow belongs, for a time.

BEAUTIFUL LOFTY THINGS

I

A Jacob's tin of luggage padlocks,
keyrings, fusewire, split-pins,
wingnuts and washers; unboxed
glockenspiel; stacks of yellowed
90s *Times of India*; a son's guitar
and VOX amp; BMX handlebar
pads; Nikon tripod; pharmacist's
locked Victorian cabinet; an uncle's
birds'-eye-maple escritoire; another's
darkroom reels and drum; full cast-list
of *papier-maché* Punch & Judy heads;
ballet pumps; Ponchielli's *Dance
of the Hours* when you unclick
a lacquered jewel box; plus unsold
stocks of my father's book on 'time'.

II

And this battered cardboard box of hours,
of every clock that ever failed the test
of time, the clocks that time forgot,
whose *wingèd chariots* outran –
or flew backwards as one did,
once, chillingly. Superannuated
digitals with plugs cut off.
Or gnawed-away inside, corroded
by their flaky single-cells.
                                    And
one that pulses on, its scarlet
twelve-colon-zero-zero frozen
at Gary Cooper's analog *High Noon*,
the pumpkin minute, Yeats's
stroke of midnight, good Doctor Faust's
Mephistophlean hour come
round, its still unanswered
blink still shrugging *Che sera, sera*.

TIME ENOUGH

i.m. Cahal A. Dallat (1921-2007)

Not one for *they'll-carry-me-out* pronouncements, but slow to quit the second house long after he was no longer fit: best of his acquisitions already in the Castle Street Museum, the remnant, beachcomber finds he'd not now polish to 'stones', ash-plants that would never make walking canes, two-pint milk containers hoarded for some acrylic art-class purpose, collectively rendering the wood-shed unusable. But when we found he'd rigged-up his folding artist's chair and easel above the pool from a leaky double radiator so he could still paint in the kitchen where light lasted late, we knew there was plenty to do, but time enough to do it in.

Easy-going West Coast shark-fishers on our holiday hotel's front summerseat had, decades back, ribbed him for his restless Northern go, his packing waders, binoculars, tourist guides and seven Aran-jumpered children into a family station wagon, to hit another headland, famine pier, sandbank, an arch made from a whale's rib: *When God made time*, they'd say in their leisurely fashion, *He made plenty*.

That last Sunday we took the shore route by the caravan park his brother had owned, to where Marconi sent his first marine signals, to the cooled volcanic geology he loved as much as history. Back over the bridge his father built he nodded left: *I might be headed there soon*, like he meant the secondary school he'd headmastered, long since sold for council offices.

But he meant the next-along care home. A glimpse of light. A turning point. A signal.

Always telling us to slow our own restless energies, he parted with the shark-men's line, the *time* and *God* thing he'd taken on board with pride and a shade of irritation way back. But he ended it, not with *plenty* but, *He made enough*.

Time for sibling texting when we get back to town. Time to make his lone life easier at last, we said.

Time, though, wasn't on our side. Monday phone calls flurried. And he was gone before we'd time to pack, time to drive back up to the coast. Maybe always knew he'd know when he'd had enough. Had plenty.

SOUTH CHINA MORNING POST

Like poking the last-place's uninhabited
wasps' nest into a Do-It-All binbag,
safebreaking Captain Higgs's Royal
Navy steamer-trunk in the cellar
was both essence of trepidation
and an onus that brooked no deferral –
though bearing in mind the much-minded
matter of dog-remains at the prior address
I cautioned the kids to stay put
at the stone steps' top while I took
the family jemmy to the hasps.
                              Absence
has its own kinds of presence but cellar,
chest, indeed Clarence Higgs himself
would hold no fear over us everafter.
                              Our eldest
shouldered, unbeknownst to us, the role
of the erstwhile captain's unremunerated –
and positively posthumous – batman/PA.

Downstairs first to sort morning posts,
secretly RSVP-ing Kowloon Jockey Club
invites, forging a nautical scrawl,
nurturing ties with the archipelago,
declining Lucky Star Dating Agency profiles,
while accepting endless village honours.

And dabbling with the captain's stocks –
put it no stronger – on the Hang Seng,
watching the Nikkei Dow, building
a startling futures portfolio that,
he assures us, all had settlement dates
months, weeks, hours anyway, before
the momentarily seismic Kobe tremors
and the whole 'rogue trader' fall-out.

MALCOLM

Ok, so don't give me
all that, 'artificial intelligence' –
can you tell a debit from a credit?

This much, the minute I settled
in the *Quinquecento's* passenger seat,
outside Oxford station, Rexine
briefcase on knees, feet
kept out of the car's dog bowl.
                            Malcolm's
idea of *keeping you going,*
of getting on like a house on fire.

As we did after a casual fashion.

Our own business years later,
project meetings, sales visits,
technology conferences together,
the second last, one Sunday
in a vast Midlands exhibition hangar,
his first attempt to get back to work
months after the op.
                        He wound
me up over the red desk-lamp
with a supposed long-life bulb,
that I bought, that penultimate joint-
outing, from an exhibitor's stand.

That would outlive him, that bulb,
by nearly 30 years and counting.

GIANT

The one exceptional thing about him –
as we worked late August nights on import
software for Italian racing bikes for his friend Italo,
percentage landing charges, demurrage, lire
conversions and freight forwarding –

was there was nothing exceptional about him
if you ignored the tallest-man-in-the-country
thing, maybe in-the-world back then, and maybe
his giant-size civility. And that we'd take
our son to watch him at Sunday soccer

though basketball was his first love, or to see
him play a circus giant in the Merrick film.
(Yes, in-the-world, probably – a Melbourne chain
had him open 'giant' hypermarkets across that huge
continent). And that his VW driver's seat

was well in the back, his racing-bike a pair
of penny-farthing 'pennies' with eleven gears.
Our children found out giants today
far from overbearing could be wry,
awkward and funny – like, but not at all

like, anybody else. And even when he sat
right down on our low-profile sofa
he couldn't avoid talking down to us.
The papers when he finally passed on
would focus mostly on the ten pallbearers.

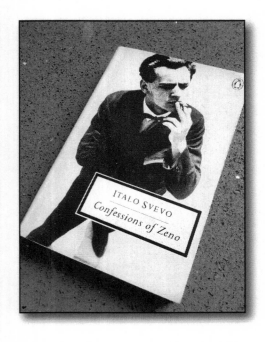

HORSE

This England is So Different —
ITALO SVEVO
onetime resident of Charlton Church Lane

The huge head lies across the pavement
outside the Chinese, one large blinkered
eye unblinking, Zeno's millet-bag scattered

and the rag-and-bone cart's swag
– a Baby Belling, telly, and a small spin dryer –
tumbled, strewn in our midsummer roadway

all down the steep hill that could crack
a noble heart. Still awesome, the head,
as those I could see inside a dark forge

en route to the tanyards daily, or snorting,
shivering, whinnying, at our fencewire
with Willie Parker insisting they loved

stroking, could sense your fear.
I'm back among cavalry
at Balaklava, Gettysburg, at Agincourt

as the totter mutters on about how he'd
be put to some great and unnecessary expense
to get the bleedin' horse shifted, and no mistake.

AUNT CYNTHY DALLETT

ay up there all alone," said Abby Pendexter. "I'm no hand
f alone, an' I had it before me, so I really got to dread it. I
njoy it after I get there, seein' Aunt Cynthy, an' she's
o much better than I expect to find her."

we'll start early," said Mrs. Hand cheerfully; and so
ted. As Miss Pendexter went down the foot-path to
she sent grateful thoughts back to the little sitting-room
st left.

oors are opened!" she exclaimed to herself. "Here I've
or an' distressed at beginnin' the year with nothin', as
t I couldn't think o' even goin' to make poor old Aunt
riendly call. I'll manage to make some kind of a little
o, an' somethin' for dear Mis' Hand. 'Use what you've
r always used to say when every sort of an emer-
up, an' I may only have wishes to give, but I'll make
es!"

II

THE ENGLISH LESSON OF
MY AUNT CYNTHIE

In England we do not have agreement. *Naturellement*.
As the words used to epithet in England are neutral.
Also in England adjectives are non-pluralitsic.
Due to our history *we* is constitutionally singular.

And *you* is plural, rendering *you is* a solecism.
As in *Bess you is my woman now* by George
and Ira who are not English and thus unreliable.
Try to remember in England that *you* can be plural.

In numerous idiolects surrounding this sceptred thingy
a strictly improper if useful distinction is made
between *you* and *yous* as in, but unlike, the French.
Or *yeez* and *y'all* in rebellious colonial states.

In China the Mandarin class have a nicely distinguished
diction to indicate caste, which strictures have never applied
this side of the jolly multitudinous seas incarnadine, *eg*
a word in your pink and shell-like old son – know what I mean?

But the words to describe in England are simple itself.
We are neuter, singular, non-pluralistic: one is not
obliged to consider agreement.
                              But remember the upside
of this – that in England disagreement never occurs.

AT THE MARINA HOTEL

We've lived too long with our unorthodox nun's
foretelling – *freedom will come when Muscovy men,*
skiffings of snow or hail bristling their bearcoats,
set foot in our estuary – not to feel a frisson,
Liam, Kevin and I, on the bar...

                                     as a reefer-
jacketed crew at the Cold War's height
troops into the velour residents lounge.

Gumboots off, feet up on plate-glass-topped
coffee tables. The one with Trotsky lunettes
scanning prices, translating cocktail names to
barracking laughs, and black cigarettes all round.

Toasts, then one hauls a squeezebox
from his duffle, weighs in with the strident
fourth that's *Stenka Razin*, that we know, Kevin,
Liam and me, as *The Carnival is Over*.

And when it finally is, Kevin's really
taken with them.
                        That's not a figure of speech.
Kevin is, after a long Vladivar night of the soul,
taken with them.
                        Postcard from Stavanger,
Spent All Souls on atomic-neutral beach
in Iceland. Followed up with *Detained on Nevsky*
Prospekt for anti-Soviet attitudes outside
Cathedral on Spilled Blood. And after,
nothing. *Nada. Zilch.*
                       While Liam slouches
towards another rough beast that will lour
over our next forty odd years.
                        For myself
I buy the one-row squeezebox for a night's
bar-earnings, and find the seventeenth-century nun's
prophecy had no snow-omens, just Russian
galleons hoving in to pier *with top-sails afire.*

TOUJOURS PRÊT

Our lives are Swiss
Army Knives — *so Cool*,
as once were Mont Blanc fountain
pens — knife blades, two,
folded safely into ourselves,
screwdriver for running repairs
fits all (except cross-head, Pozidriv) — then gouger-
spike-bore-augur-bradawl,
pre-war bean-tin opener,
(can seriously damage user).

Point six, the necessity of bottle-opening:
EU standard corkscrew or, UK,
lever for prising crown caps —
though an infantry that favours bottled *pilsner*
over ring-pulls or Grolsch's porcelain bung,
rubber washer and spring, takes cool too far.

Plus, indispensable —
for today's horseman —
hoof-extricating gadget:

And, on crimson ground
the simple white cross
forever intervenes!

CAPTURING MAIN STREET

Off the track-less-beaten
this far you just can't tell
is that a lonesome train whistle
or yodelling Jimmy Rogers

breaking on the octave,
but you'll find the drugstore sign
unchanged: *ESTD. 1910.*
Where, notwithstanding this

winter's flu-jab posters,
it could still be a junction
Bonnie & Clyde shot through,
or all the Joads lit out from.

In familiar gloom
an authentic full-size family
poses at the soda-fountain
outstaring rubberneckers: you order

root-beer splits, for Doc,
for *The Last Picture Show*, for
all our matinees.
              And check
there isn't, beyond the booths,

a pleased-with-himself Vermeer
of small-town life, with paintbrush,
bow tie, and clenched briar, grinning
behind his *Saturday Evening Post* easel.

DUXTON HOTEL

Just 3 desk/shelf photos of you since
we stopped mounting snaps in albums,
and before we uploaded them cloud-wise
to be scarcely – in the last how many
years – ever viewed.
      In elegant black
with the nouveau Adam & Eve pendant,
looking out over Stephen's Green
from a Shelbourne window.
        Tousled
in sunlight one Leith evening,
early two-thousands perhaps?

And once in 'tropical white',
mango and pomegranates on the table,
in a split-level, verandah'd room
after we'd sampled Singapore's
outrageous *Slings* and emerged
to cloudbursts and hailings of rickshaws.

On a long drenched haul back
to Old Town, after talk of weather,
you ask our ageing, sinewed pedaller
through veils of rain if
he's always done this.
     All my life,
he says, *except when the Japanese came
and I was prisoned as coolie to build their fort.*

THE AUNT WHO

whistled, despite its much-quoted
tearjerk effect on Our Lady.
                              The one
with just three songs: *The Man who Broke
the Bank* (Joyce hauled that song sheet
Europe-wide in his pasteboard valise
– everywhere in fact but *Monte Carlo*),
then *When they Begin the Beguine* and *Beware
my Foolish Heart*.
                    That always aunt
who was there to walk us to Bertucelli's.
To the pier, or Marconi's. Was there to bake
macaroni cheese in her Wellington Park
apartment between my autumn lectures.

The selfsame aunt who had, everyone knew,
in her day, declined repeated pleadings for
her hand from the dashing affluent heir
to a prominent road-building contractor
sometime between two wars.
                            At one
of the 'Great' hotels, 'Northern', 'Southern',
'Western' perhaps.
                    No one, it seemed,
had ever been able to say for sure.

JOHN SHERRARD GILLIGAN

As embroidered on his inside hatbands. And not just the one he wore giving away his daughter (in my parents' wedding snaps) but headgear he sported daily.

Though not a punitive day, heaven knows, hardly a day's work at all. At his counting-house leather desk by ten-thirty, home for cooked dinner, back downtown for three. Believed Corporation conductors clipped his ticket with more *kudos* when he adopted the 1930 ad's advice, *If you want to get ahead, get a hat.*

Saw himself, I guessed, as proof of that getting-ahead: Irish-speaking clerk in the 1901 census, postwar wine-shop cashier, newly wed in a new Falls Road terrace, *Lisheen* on the gate for the Canon Sheehan novel they still read in *plucky little Catholic Belgium.*

Managed a whole distillery by '28. Approaches in Borsalinos from heavyset Sicilian gentlemen on SS *Majestic* to New York. Again at Penn Station. And again after last mass at Brooklyn's Saint Rose of Lima. All a step or two, he thought, from his Sligo father's Smithfield spirit-grocers. All put down to that six-and-seven-eighths homburg.

All due in turn, perhaps, to growing up in his mother's hat-shop (her mother's before her) on the same Smithfield sidestreet as his father's winery, the millinery business retained, rarely for patriarchal Victorian Belfast, in her own name: 'Ann-Jane Duffin: Cap Manufacturer'. Who once told my ninety-something-now godfather, then a tall wide-eyed five-year-old, *mightily impressed* and seated at her bed's end, of the failed Presbyterian rising. *I know how rebellious and stiff-necked you are* the Lord chided us in Deuteronomy.

And of her own great-uncle hidden with Henry Joy on Slemish Mountain until he was sold, betrayed, and marched to Ballymena's Moat one June Friday, hatless. Just a golden hemp-rope adorning that fine, stiff, Sherrard neck.

UTTERANCES

It's when I ask at Marché aux Puces (ostensibly
buying up *cartons et papiers d'antan* but the jaunt's
a cover for studying four-fingered styles of Manouche
swing-musette around Porte de Clignancourt braziers),

when I ask in a feast of enunciation *Combien* –
ça coûte – cette boite de 'Marmite Cubes'? and the *vendeur*
rasps in Marlboro English O, *say it again,*
je just adore le francais with a North Antrim accent,

that I see my grandfather at a table-clothed Bayreuth terrace,
lavishing his Ballynafeigh spirit-grocers' proceeds
on inter-war Sekt, tentatively asking the maestro
of a silver thirty-piece band between intermezzos,

Haben sie, 'The Londonderry Air', *bitte?* to hear,
Mais oui, of course, sir, everyone knows 'Danny Boy'.

HOW IT WAS

Coming back he wanted it all
to have been whiff of Gitanes,
Place du Tertre silhouettes, *carnets*
de billets and Clignancourt jazzers:
but in truth it was neither
the *cité* nor the heart-stopping
Hovercraft ride but a long dark
northbound night, L'Île de France,
the Artois, where they'd stared every
few leagues at something they'd never
before seen, genuine Pinocchio
Pleasure Islands of incandescence
au bord de l'Autoroute.
                              Later
they would tire of service areas,
even those in *Pays Bas* or Austria.
And anyway this time their coach driver
took them off-road to a local
tavern by Arras's serried dead ranks
where they drank smaller coffees
than they'd ever seen before, beneath
the baleful gaze of two black wolves
and embarked gratefully
for the kilometres ahead,
her sleeping, ruby-ringed hands in his.

L'ORCHESTRE À BRETELLES

He knows: that the stretch for Yanks
is between St Paul and George V
on Vincennes-Neuilly, the yellow *ligne six*;

that *les flics* will take the *kepi* of euros
and dollar bills if they catch him
on the train but he doesn't have a permit
for the glazed cavernous halls either;

that *I Love Paris* is mere Hollywood
pastiche of Menilmontant's *tzigane* minor,
not a patch on *Indifference, Tico-Tico,*
Perles de Cristal, even *Baker Street*...
                              though it works
in the Nikolaiviertel, Charles Bridge, too,
wherever Mid-Westerns go;
                              knows he should work
the captive faces in the crowd before
the brake-hiss announces the next
station of the Metro
                    but it is here
in unlit tunnels that his lighted reflection
lets him switch off sound and marvel
in double-layered Metro-carriage windows
at a seeming stranger's fingers
flickering impossibly
                    repeatedly,
over pearlised buttons as in the first
silent movie ever made, its ironical
subject a Parisian *accordeoniste*.

Stolzenfels Castle, Koblenz, Germany

SCHLOSS STOLZENFELS

He'd wondered ever since what it was about,
the night he'd walked alone at seventeen

from Rhens to Koblenz, twenty-one kilometres
round trip, on the edge of reason, the very edge

of foolishness, through a steep dramatic gorge
with its thundering autobahn, and two rail-tracks

with regular one-hundred-truck freight trains,
and a whole heaving Rhine of coal-and-steel barges;

wondered what made him sneak out of the student hostel
while others slept after the frantic evening

at the hospital with a classmate's injured hand,
what made him bring wife and children back years on,

with high-talk of freeloading on Lorelei tourist barges,
being plied with *schnapps* as he played a bar-piano,

the Konigsbacher *brauerei* with plate-glass windows
and huge Alsatians where he'd shared a watchman's

midnight bread and *bratwurst*, the castle you might see
cloaked inhabitants scale by moonlight. But what

it was really about only clicked, decades later.
Simply the first time ever no one in the world

had even the remotest idea where he might be.

AFTER

Ľudovít Fulla,
Slovak National Gallery, Bratislava

Noon, a dry-tongued heat
after the obligatory castle morning.

A torn-out travel writer's grudging
account – rough folded in our guide –
finds fault with, he complains,
too-Eastern-bloc housing blocks,
over *der schönen blauen* Danube,
too numerous post-Communist
ticket-stub-tearers; too-religious
Christs on varnished street-corner
oak crosses; even too-Western
pizzerias, a busker playing
I Just Called…
                    All that
intersectionality, that excitement
being exactly what we've come
to find in a visited-for-the-first-time
European capital city.

But all that's as nothing to three
enchanted things in a dim
afternoon Esterházy Palace:

Janosik, the local, the true,
Robin Hood on horseback; a vivid
trumpeter soaring over ploughmen,
reapers, farm carts; a small red
mother and child
                    weaving seamlessly
through Cubism, socialist realism,
folk art and Byzantine orthodoxy,
as if they'd been there all along.

THE TIME IT TAKES

In less than the time it takes Chris to give me what he swears won't be short-back-and-sides, I get the ins-and-outs of the Mini Cooper his father bought cash-in-hand and clearly clocked outside Shepherd's Bush Market to take them down the Old Kent Road and Brenner Pass *…no Mont Blanc yet, we came over long before Makarios, before Grivas and EOKA B…*

I divide my barbering equally between both sides though Javid over-the-road insists it wasn't like Ireland, shouldn't have been partitioned, like Macmillan said, Greeks and Turks on the same streets in Larnaca, in Nicosia, more like both sides on the same Haringay Ladder streets today.

By which time Chris is past Split, father staring at tractor taillights doing 15 kph with an alfalfa-stacked trailer Dutch-barn high, seventeen hours out of Calais, and they're still nineteen minimum from Piraeus, with another thousand kilometres by boat before they get to Limassol for the Holy Theophany, so that when I look down now on lit isolated farmsteads in snow-skiffed mountains (Macedonia, Albania?) two hours out from Larnaca on a four-hour night flight to Heathrow, I swear those are the dimly flickering lights of a trying-to-pass 1962 Mini whose alternator's on the blink, days from 'home' or 'back home', and I think of meze and bread, and barbers.

BACK ISSUES

Put the *Observers* and *Spectators*
by the *Stands* with a view of the finish,
at least within sight of *Horizons:*
place *Guardians* by the front door,
Private Eyes under the eaves
60s Practical Mechanics in the shed,

not omitting a single *Iota*.
Tablets and various *Supplements*
belong in the mirrored cabinet, your
teen-scene *Petticoats* in the dressing-up box.
Forget lost *Fortnights*, missed *Prospects*,
but keep all the back numbers of *Life*.

New Yorkers go in the loft-space,
(cold-water walk-up), *The Reader*
in here with our books, *Writing*
Women in the sun-trap gazebo I guess,
but don't take your eyes, for a moment
off those old student-days' *Honest Ulstermen*.

TIN WHISTLE

Not penny whistle, I tell the CNN
anchor, *tin whistle* – before playing
The Foggy Dew in a Kansas City Irish Fest
segment that's spiked later for more urgent
Hillary-news.
            Always tin whistle,
since, say, the days a young
Charles Causley packed his
pre-war model in a navy knapsack
for Scapa Flow, Belfast, Freetown,

the one I played through a long summer:
found tucked away at the back
of his desk. Now in a glass case: part
of a fellow poet-musician's shelf-life.

This, on the other hand, is the one America
might have heard on CNN
from sea to shining sea, that
I've played off-air from Lubec, anyway,
to New Orleans, Carmel, Seattle,
and like the peripatetic Oliver
Goldsmith, from Marseille to Venice.

And once at a massive wedding
above Jaipur where Arup's auntie
asked for *The Salley Gardens* and then,
as always in India, told her tale of Holborn,
LSE in the thirties, then the Republic,
her husband's assassination, a Kalashnikov-ed
guard at her side for 30 years now.

You must recite us your Mr Yeats. Not
that sentimental 'Innisfree', those 'Cloths
of Heaven'. What we want is 'The ghost
of Roger Casement, knocking at the door.'

COLLECTIVES

Abandonments of agricultural implements,
a desolation of lean-tos,
ruinations of end walls and door jambs,
a weed-kingdom of once-formal week-ending borders.

Evanescences of studio poses,
a misapprehension of nemeses,
an excise or fondness of distillings,
spendthriftings of dollars from Mirabeau, Michigan.

Arrivals of stretch-Hertz-limos
a paparazzi of Pentaxes
high babble of explorations
unearthings of hill-dwellers' lost kitchen-middens.

A collaging of willow-plate shards,
incomprehensions of butter querns,
a glossolalia of townland nomenclatures,
burgeonings of interpretive heritage centres.

A pride of roots,
parliaments of rooks,
exaltations of gulls,
a shoal of cod.

SUCH SWEET SORROW

She leaves him without a word, *senza*
una single dictionary entry, not the earthliest
chance of a capacious one like the 58-letter
Anglesey village (upon which he might build
a whole new alphabet, lexicon, civilisation,
perhaps)
        or the essentially donnish
floccinaucinihilipilification
though the *habit of making little* might well
be cited as probable cause.

                Too much
to expect *À bientôt, Arrividerci, Auf Wiedersehen*
— without the pet terms of endearment —
(just half the dictionary page of foreign
words in everyday use), even a *Laters!*,
all with their formal implication
of *someday, one day*.

              A monosyllable
would've done. *Love* a touch too much
to hope for. *'Bye* could've worked
but no.
        She left him without a word,
unlettered, unutterably wordless.

THE WITNESSES

Wednesday morning, Arnolfini Gallery, Bristol

Not having bothered – having even mulled over –
forking out for the telescopic service-area
                                  selfie-stick
he finds he has to stretch his short arm
                          this far
to take in all of his blue velvet D-J,
                            his nights-in-
white-satin South-East-Asian bride, her matron-
of-honour half-sister,
                and his best
mate (could be a much-older brother)
outside the glinting portico:
                    far enough out
to lose the close-up convex convict look.
                         Meaning
they'll have only hiked all the way down
Narrow Quay from *Births, Marriages & Deaths*
in such finery to find an august portico
                        suited
to the solemnization of wedding selfies,
if he can only get the zoom right and
                      miss
the two doorway reflections he won't be able
                         to crop later.

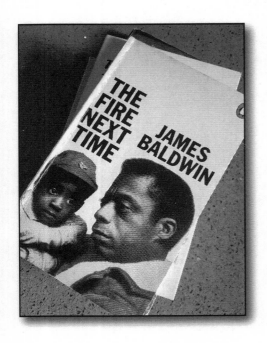

THE FIRE NEXT TIME

Hard to credit now his mouthing flame,
dancing on live coals in the yard
where a draggled ex-Chipperfields' lion
lolled, stretched, the year before,
hard to acknowledge the Huck-Finn-style
wild-man act could still seem seemly a century on
in a town we'd heard welcomed
wartime troops, including the sideman
who'd passed off on my father an unuseable
Austro-Hungary-pitch soprano sax
our *desafinado* link to both
Bartok and Bechet.
                Hard to believe
this long, unpublished – buried, even,
by an editor sensitive to criticism, wary
of gifting the Fascists 'black' propaganda –
this copperplate letter in the Herald's archive:
a coloured GI imploring our Christian people
to refrain from calling them names
in the street; a man beginning to doubt
the Allied cause he's here to fight for.

PIT

Nearer my town than yours,
on the downhill stretch when I'd hike
the sixteen miles home by night,
a gravel pit, or maybe sand,
derrick and conveyors long oxidised,
we'd pass without seeing ourselves
children of a lost industrial era,
your bauxite-mining great-grandfather,
my shirtsleeved grandfather on top of
a coal-mine's giant pulley-wheels
in a nineteen-hundred-and-something
Town-Museum display.

A quarry we'd passed for years
un-seeing until after the birthday
we bought the Nikon FM
and you took black-and-white roll after roll,
watched images emerge through developer,
stop-bath, fixer, in our London
cellar, until we finally understood it
as relic, icon,
                a page
of romanticised history, long before
we knew of Salgado, the Rust Belt,
or the creakings of vanquished Mexborough.

NAMING

I'd done the interview, located
the *Yorkshire Grey* in Theobald's Road –
a Fullers, where Harry Gold led with
that man-high bass sax his *Pieces of Eight* –
while you sought out silk-hatted city
messengers, in heats we'd not dreamed
impinged in subtemperate isles.
                             Cool
to change at Earls Court to cheesecloth,
open-toeds, and out to Castelnau;
communal paths, number nine's bean-rows,
'the Rec', and your English aunt's fresh hake
her Sid bought from Limassol Takis's taxi-shelter
off the Broadway.
                     In a lull between family trees,
cousins' LSE Masters, Lonsdale Belts and follow-up
A-sides, he threaded a hand-labelled reel
onto a Grundig, the room suddenly rich
in fugitive light with your mother's lost
voice, sheer essence of dancehall longing
before all manner of things would cease to be
well: *a capella* but not *heavenly shades
of night or palms or Oh, you railroad
stations!* of her girlhood but softly, softly,
What must be, must be.
                          Remember,
she bargained absently, in that echoey
formica-topped 'Sixties scullery
to name one muchacha for me. So we did.

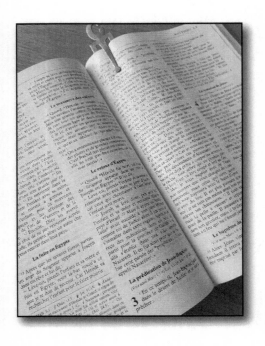

RENDER UNTO

At school, when we did the temptations
it wasn't only the pinnacle
but the thought of seraphim swooshing
lest Jesus's heel be grazed,
dashed on rose-red petra.
My granny's Geneva bible
had *heurter* – to *collide* – not *dash*,
like our pebbledash garage wall
and the grey convent houses above.

Dash is palpable – when, free-floating,
candescent with exhaust gas and sparks
our station-wagon sashays and cannons
against roughcast central barriers
after a careening Alfa cabriolet
rockets us into a tailspin
as in an earlier poem but
literal not allegorical now: not
that it signifies much when steering
– like life – is out of my hands.

Not that it counts as we throttle
– not up the wrong side this time but –
back down the fast lane on our side
to face the batallions of halogens
snapping at us: and we reach each
for the other's hand, no time
to say, even think, *after all these…*
or view our flashpast biopics.

No: sooner the Cassidy-Sundance
Bolivia gambit; or Thelma
& Louise giving it shoe; or one
of either or both; there is only –
space, time slowed to a long
fermata, the baton suspended
at that raised Cyclopian eyebrow.
and these words, *heurter, angels* and *dash…*

DAYBOOK

Grandfathers didn't go in goal back then, do headers or keepy-uppies, or uncles' sleight-of-hand with Zippo lighters, or the one where a silver dollar walks across nicotined knuckles, pops from under an ear-lobe.

But I smiled, almost, once, at my Dallat grandfather, and his poker-faced entries in brass-bound ledgers my father had stacked in our loft: how many bricks per day, in stubby carpenter's pencil, which doctor's semi on the town's northern avenues was redecorated, who got paid short that week: and suddenly *VE Day, no work, mass twice* (only business and religious observances permitted in the daybook).

Then late that summer, *VJ Day, no work* (wasn't Hiroshima worth a mass?).

Same terseness in his burials ledger: *Stoddart Moore* (no hint he was the town's poet) or *Lizzie Dallat*, date, but no clue that she was his niece. Then in war years so many *Known-unto-Gods* washed up at Jackson's Pool, Marconi's, or Carraig Uisneach. All interred in pre-Reformation – thus pre-denominational – Bonamargy Friary ruins, east of the rivermouth.

Then this: *severed head collected at Port Na Spaniagh, buried in Bonamargy, Tuesday.* Of forensics, or investigation, of theological concerns about the resurrection of the body, glorious and complete, not a single, blunt, stubby-pencilled word.

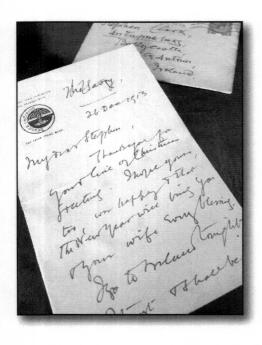

DE-ANGLICIZATION

I

Sir Roger writing on Irish-made notelets,
from the Chilterns home of a friend
whose name he'll use briefly as alias
when captured.
　　　　　　But that Good Friday is two
years ahead: for now all is goodwill.
　　　　　　　　　　Knighted
as the first humanitarian *rapporteur*, he sends
Stephen's Day greetings to my grandfather's
Ann Street neighbour, Stephen Clarke,
instructor in the woodcarving industry
Roger's Protestant friends have created
for the town.
　　　　　　I go to Ireland
tonight + shall be with FJB at Ardrigh
during part of January. Mrs Newman
is at Reading – and for the rest we are both
well and often busy for Ireland.

II

In the 1960s my uncle, campaigning
for electoral reform (and impressed still
by his grandmother's tale of a hanging),
meets with Fenner Brockway
a Pentonville CO half a century
earlier when Sir Roger was condemned;

who watched through bars a warder
escort his charge back from an eve-of-execution
stroll across the yard where his bones would lie
for 50 years;
　　　　　　who saw the prisoner stop
to inhale that same blue August sky
that hesitated for a second over Magherintemple,
over Ballycastle, over Murlough.

A SAXOPHONE IN AMBER

Watching the scrappy marriage-band
in Satyajit Ray's *Pather Panchali*
on their *Long* tuneless *Way to Tipperary*,
post-colonially British in its ersatz Irishness,
I'm back years, in Tech Block C15,
New Okhla Industrial Development Area,
the daily procession below bomb-proof windows
of bicyclists head-carrying entire forests,
rickshaw pedallers with a dozen schoolkids
hugging tiffin tins on a rickety plank,
near-comatose white noonday cows.

And afternoons:
disbanding marriage-bandsmen
in white uniforms with gold and scarlet
braid unloosed, tubas, trombones,
slung over shoulders, under arms,
and the occasional exuberant
shimmering trumpet cadenza.
                              Silver
instruments, not brass; red keywork;
not abandoned by a vanished empire
but new and locally forged.
                              Irresistible,
then, when I meet a local maker
casting keys and levers in noon-dark
archways below Amber Fort,
                              this silver
circussy soprano with the wrong mouthpiece –
but yes, the red-enamelled keys –
and a tone hovering
                      between *Alpenhorn*
and classical *chennai*, braying, perfect
for our *desafinado* post-colonial revelries.

MUSLIM SAINT

Not an easy Delhi day, twisted
ankle at Lal Qila (wrecked metatarsal,
they'd find, in London a month after)
                                    and a *tuk-tuk*
driver spotting helplessness, abandoning
itinerary, Humayun's Tomb, Chandni Chowk,
et al, contrives to take in, well off-plan,
emporia *where best sahibs go.*
                        Relenting
(I'm close to feverish) when one offers icy Coke
on a verandah, I part with *rupee*
for this Muslim saint painted by the patron's
only brother, who's just that year, come first
in Mrs Ghandi's All-India Painting Contest.
I'm paying for the painting, and the prize.

Back at Nirula's Hotel with my left foot
in minibar ice that night I learn one
of the Midlands team has bought an identical
hand-painting from a merchant whose only brother
also won this year's first prize, it seems,
a stallholder in Delhi's 'Covent Garden', chic
Haus Khas, completely different part of town.

ON NOT PUTTING ON DEAD MEN'S SHOES

When someone's mother's brother
my father knew at the seminary next the jail
did his *bildungsroman* thing in Malibu
and borrowed the insurance-exec's
impenetrable poem-title, we weren't long
discovering the muscular Havana-roller
and his 'concupiscent' *gelati* –
the rooting out of concupiscence
being a thing much to be desired
in my father's mother's prayerbook –

though it wasn't *wenches in such*
dress that got me, but the *horny feet*
beneath the sheet with fantails,
not stockinged like those our forefathers
Daguerrotyped for friends in Boston
or those the Feds snapped to show
the fifty-caliber hail really had
taken-out Pancho or Jesse big-time
or Emiliano, say; *bless*
his little coffin socks:

more like Che who exited barefoot,
a roll-out freezer-shelf corpse
in a noir-ish Nordic procedural,
like Mantegna's Christ our daughter
took us to see in La Brera:
as sudden feet protrude
from a saffron-and-gold shroud
on a bamboo-poled litter
shouldered at the head of
a straggled Sunday cortege

that passes this Easter morning
the Church of the Five Precious Wounds
en route to Nigam Bodh Ghat
(off the Ring Road past Lal Qila)
with its Yamuna firewood piles.

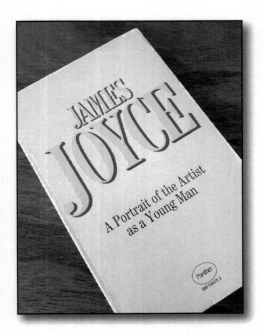

MISS FOGARTY

Absurd to make a Joycean thing of it
in terms of *bildungsroman* or
home-town political shenanigans
but our one-room Public Library
shared its space with the Court
of Petty Sessions, placing the literary act
in a judicial context, subtly raising
bibliographic misdemeanours – damage, fines,
inappropriate selections – to the level
of the poachers and minor rebels
who – we could read in the *Northern
Constitution* – had been processed through
that shared municipal experience.

I'd read all of *Portrait* at twelve and knew
I'd verged on material that, had Miss
Fogarty (first name Jean, I once heard,
her father the bowler-hatted clerk
to the Urban District Council, a brother
brewing *mate* and salvation in dark Peru)
been on duty when I'd had it stamped out,
her unofficial censorship would have
avoided this *impasse*, her role being
the stamping out of precisely that sort of thing.

With those oak doors you couldn't peek
to see if it was her or the less-clued-up
deputy: and they'd have heard you clump
up the bare stairs with a pile of hardbacks
anyway.
            Even if you'd a Davin or Cranly
to engage her in erudite misdirection
it wouldn't do to slip it back on the shelves
as without due process, missives about fines
would assuredly find their way from the County
to the borrower's home address, words
with the *paterfamilias* ensuing.
                        The very essence
of a moral scruple that Joyce fellow would
have tied his *inwit* in knots with for sure.

SPAGHETTI

Kinda tumbleweed mood hung around
Antrim Arms Corner, the Royal Hotel lounge,

not just that someone's uncle hijacked
a police Cortina with a stout-bottle's neck

in his pocket-lining thrust *Reservoir-Dogs*-style
against the sergeant's spine (not one

you'd have tried a year or two on, when
things fell apart), but the way old-time 'youths' –

teenagers *avant-la-lettre* with leather
elbow-patch sportscoats – adopted aliases:

Bosco, Cisco, Amigo, The Shadow,
all matinee-Western-inspired advances

on a previous generation's monickers
when *Bantam* and *Sparrow* ruled the roost

in the Snowy Mountain squad, all clocking-
in at the car plant by the time I grew up.

Kinda feeling you wouldn't play
twenty-one with your back to the door, would never

eyeball them but made sure they couldn't
imply you'd ignored them. You could still

slide a whiskey-straight a glass-top bar's
length or wear a bullet-holed dollar

on your watch chain, if you had a waistcoat,
all this before the shooting started,

before the bad, the ugly years, the spaghetti.

Acknowledgements

Acknowledgement for first publication is due to the editors of *Ploughshares, Ocean State Review, North, Keats-Shelley Newsletter, Big City Lit, All That Jazz, Aldeburgh Poetry Paper, Winchester Anthology, Slovakia in Poems* and *Southword*.

"Giant" won the 2017 Keats-Shelley Poetry Prize, and "Collectives," "Miss Fogarty," "Schloss Stolzenfels" and "On Not Putting on Dead Men's Shoes" were prizewinners or shortlisted/commended in London Writers Prize, the Gregory O'Donoghue Prize, the Winchester Poetry Prize and the Torbay Poetry Competition respectively.

Thanks are due to The Society of Authors, Tor House Foundation (Carmel, California), Heinrich Böll Association (Achill Island, County Mayo), Charles Causley Trust (Launceston, Cornwall) and Lenoir-Rhyne University (Hickory, North Carolina), for providing writing time, place and inspiration.

Born in Ballycastle, County Antrim, poet, musician and critic CAHAL DALLAT lives in London where he is founder/organiser of the WB Yeats Bedford Park Project and a regular contributor to BBC Radio 4's *Saturday Review*. Winner of both Strokestown International and Keats-Shelley poetry prizes, he has recently been Charles Causley Centenary Writer/Musician-in-Residence at Causley's former Cornwall home, Research Fellow at Harry Ransom Center, University of Texas in Austin, and joint Writer-in-Residence (with Anne-Marie Fyfe) at Lenoir-Rhyne University, North Carolina. Previous poetry collections include *The Year of Not Dancing* (Blackstaff). www.cahaldallat.com

salmonpoetry

Cliffs of Moher, County Clare, Ireland

"Publishing the finest Irish and international literature."
Michael D. Higgins, President of Ireland